BORN OF THE GOSPEL

"If there come ANY unto you, and bring not THIS DOCTRINE, receiveth him not into your house, neither bid him God speed; for he that biddeth him God speed is partaker of his evil deeds." {II Jn.10, 11}

Moreno Dal Bello

BORN OF THE GOSPEL

Despite a religious climate replete with false teachers and false teachings, most who name the name of Jesus are sincerely convinced in their belief that they have the truth and are truly born again heaven-bound Christians. Their lives are filled with Bible reading, Church-going, prayer times and many other religious exercises. They talk *'jesus'* all day long and love to meet with others who *'love jesus',* too. Yet there is one very peculiar trait common among most professing christians today and that is the very sad and disturbing fact that they cannot define and, in most cases, have never actually heard God's True Gospel. Perhaps of even more concern is the tragic fact that most who profess to know God, who *have* heard the Gospel and say they believe it remain convinced that they were truly born again *before* they ever heard it. This, in spite of the fact that the Bible clearly teaches that a true believer, that is, a born again believer, a new creature in Christ, is born of the Seed of God, His Word. This booklet will show clearly from the pages of God's Holy Scriptures that the new creature in Christ springs from the Seed of God, His Holy Gospel Message, and that the life of the true believer **begins at the Gospel** and does not eventually lead one to it; that none can truly claim to be of God if they have never heard His Gospel, for **IT** is the power and wisdom of God unto Salvation.

"**...Verily, verily, I say unto thee, except a man be born again, he cannot see the Kingdom of God"** (Jn. 3:3). When the Lord Jesus Christ informed Nicodemus the Pharisee, in John 3, that a man needs to be born again in order to see the Kingdom of God, He was not, as Nicodemus wrongly assumed in verse 4, referring to a man's being *physically* re-born. Christ spoke of the necessity of being born again **spiritually**, of being **born from above** or **born of the Spirit**. As is the case with the procreation of man requiring the seed of man, so, too, the spiritual birth of man requires a seed. **As with any birth, spiritual birth has a beginning and needs a source.** What that Seed is, that necessary and vital ingredient to a person's being born again, and without which no man can be born again, is made perfectly clear in

Scripture. 1 Peter 1:23 tells us that every justified sinner is made spiritually alive by: **"Being born again, not of corruptible seed, but of incorruptible** (Seed)**, BY THE WORD OF GOD, which liveth and abideth forever."** Peter is here teaching that a man's being made alive unto God is not something which comes from within the realms of human ability, nor is it something which a man is enabled to do, but a man's being made alive unto God is a work performed exclusively by God without the aid of man: *"...Salvation is of the Lord"* (Jonah 2:9). **As a plant cannot will itself into being or come into existence unless it be by way and means of a seed, so, too, the spiritual creature cannot come into being unless it is by way and means of a seed.** If there is no seed there will be no plant and if there is **no Gospel** Seed there will be **no new creature** in Christ. The apostle John says that sons of God—those who believe on His name (Jn. 1:12)—are born **"...not of blood, nor of the will of the flesh, nor of the will of man, but OF GOD"** (Jn.1:13; see also 1 Cor.1:30; 1 Pet.1:21). One is not made a new creature in Christ by parental heritage; it is not something we inherit from Christian parents; man cannot *will* himself into becoming a new creature in Christ and no man can make another into this new creature. The new creature comes from one source and one source only: **the Gospel of Almighty God**. The beginning of the spiritual life of every true believer can be traced back to its place of origin: the Gospel of God. It is most important to note at this point that *"no man was ever converted by the mere effect of truth without the agency of the Holy Ghost, any more than seed germinates when laid on a hard rock".*

According to the apostle Peter there are only **two kinds of seed**: that which is **corruptible** and that which is **incorruptible**. The corruptible seed referred to in 1 Peter speaks of the seed of man by which we are born. The product of that seed, the human body, is subject to decay and corruption and will eventually die. The Christian, however, is a creature which will *not* perish, for he has been born of the **Seed of God** which is **incorruptible** and its fruit **eternal**. *"...as God is ever living, that which is produced directly by Him in the human soul, by the instrumentality of truth, may* *be expected also to live forever."* Though the body will one day die, the spiritual being which has been born of that Seed lives on, in God, forever. As one man has put it, **'*being born again, not of corruptible seed'*** carries with it the meaning *"Not by virtue of any descent from human parents."* Nothing corruptible can issue forth from God, therefore the 'corruptible' referred to here by Peter must mean 'that which man produces'. It must be pointed out that even the best a man can produce by way of religious effort, can only be described as corruptible, for **"A good tree cannot bring forth evil fruit, neither can a corrupt tree bring forth good fruit"** (Jn. 7:18; see also Psa. 39:5).

So we see, that for a man to be born again he **must** be born of that incorruptible Seed which comes from God and not from anything which proceeds from the man himself or from any other human agency. The new birth is not the result of a man's initiative but purely and solely something which God initiates **and** completes. The apostle James bears this out in the following verse of Scripture: **"Of HIS OWN WILL begat He us WITH THE WORD OF TRUTH..."** (Jas.1:18). James here tells us that it is solely because of God's will, not man's, that a new creature is born and He does this through His very Word. Peter, in 1 Peter 1, describes this *'Word'* as the **Word of God**. James defines this same medium as the **Word of Truth**. The word *'begat'* in James 1:18 is used metaphorically of spiritual birth by means of the Word of God and literally means *'to give birth to', 'to breed forth', 'to generate'* or *'to bring forth',* terms synonymous with a *beginning* or *birth*. As sin is pregnant with and brings forth death, so, too, the Word of God brings forth eternal life in those who are born of it. The Bible states that Christ Jesus has **"...abolished death, and hath brought LIFE and IMMORTALITY to light THROUGH THE GOSPEL"** (2 Tim.1:10). **God gives birth to His new creatures in Christ by means of His Word, the Gospel, and no other.** Just as there is no other name but the **name** of JESUS whereby a man is saved (Acts 4:12), so, too, there is no other **means** but the GOSPEL by which a man is saved. Thus we learn, that as with the natural birth of a man being something quite impossible unless it is by the means of man's seed (sperm or semen), so, too, the spiritual birth of a man is something which, according to the Bible, is an utter **impossibility** unless it is by the means of God's Seed which is His Word. Christ proclaimed that the only way a man can be sanctified, that is, made holy or set apart from other men unto God, is by way of the Word of God: **"Sanctify them THROUGH Thy Truth: THY WORD IS TRUTH"** (Jn. 17:17). Christ is said to have given Himself for the Church **"That He might sanctify and cleanse it with the washing of water BY THE WORD"** (Eph. 5:26). Clearly, from these two verses of Scripture we see that there is, and can be, no sanctification, no cleansing or washing without the instrumentality of the Word of Truth. Even after this brief look at the Scriptures, the evidence is resounding: Peter says a man is born again BY the Word of God; James tells us that God has begotten us WITH the Word of Truth; Paul says in 2 Timothy that Christ has brought life and immortality THROUGH the Gospel; Paul also states in 1 Corinthians that in Christ he has begotten us THROUGH the Gospel; and Christ Himself tells us that we are sanctified THROUGH the Truth. The whole work of salvation from start to finish is accomplished by means of the Word. *"It was not by external ceremonies, and not by any miraculous power on the heart, but by faithful application of Truth to the heart."* But what is this Word of God, this Word of Truth, exactly, without which no man can be born again? Is it the Bible in general which is referred to here, as some attest, or is it something more specific. The answer is found in God's Holy Word.

Further down in 1 Peter 1, we see in verse 25 precisely what this Word of God, this incorruptible Seed, actually is. Peter explains: **"But the Word of the Lord endureth forever. And this is the Word which by THE GOSPEL is preached unto you."** It could not have been made any clearer for us. In the context of this passage from 1 Peter, we learn that the incorruptible Seed described as the **Word of God** in verse 23 which liveth and abideth forever and by which a man is born again, is the **Word of the Lord** mentioned in verse 25 which endureth forever, and is no less than the very Gospel itself! There is no fancy manipulation of words here or eisegesis— a reading into the Scriptures what it plainly does not say—but is a proper exegesis and contextual rendering of what is being referred to as the incorruptible Seed, the Word of God and the Word of the Lord, and as we shall see, is supported by many other Scriptures throughout the Bible. For instance, Acts 8:4 speaks of those who went forth preaching the Gospel as they that *"...went everywhere preaching the Word"*, a phrase found in a myriad of Scriptures. The two terms are used as if they are one in Acts 8:25: **"And they, when they had testified and PREACHED THE WORD of the Lord, returned to Jerusalem, and PREACHED THE GOSPEL in many villages of the Samaritans."** The Book of Acts includes within its pages a record of the extensive preaching done by the apostles and other disciples of Christ. This preaching was often referred to as the *preaching of the Word*, or the *Word of God*, or the *Word of the Lord Jesus* or the *preaching of the Word of the Lord*. In Acts 15:7 Peter introduces a new term: **"...that the Gentiles by my mouth should hear THE WORD OF THE GOSPEL, and believe."** A similar, and more encompassing term, is used in Colossians 1:5: **"For the hope which is laid up for you in heaven, whereof ye heard before in THE WORD OF THE TRUTH OF THE GOSPEL."** The Scriptures makes it all irresistibly and abundantly clear. The Word of Truth, the Word of God, the Word of the Lord Jesus etc., are all references to THE GOSPEL of God and none can be born again without it.

James 1:18, as we have already discovered, talks of the Christian being brought forth, or given birth to, by the Word of Truth. Another key verse which lends further support to the Word of Truth being the Gospel, is found in Ephesians 1:13: **"In Whom ye also trusted, AFTER that ye heard the Word of Truth, THE GOSPEL of your salvation..."** Paul the apostle is speaking here of the Ephesians and their trust in Christ rightly being their only hope for salvation. Significantly, he states that they trusted in Christ only **after** they heard the Word of Truth which he immediately defines as being none other than the very Gospel of God, the Gospel of their salvation. We learn then from Paul's statement that none can be said to truly trust in Christ **before** they actually hear the Gospel of God, for it is only within the confines of that Gospel that Christ, and His Righteousness, is revealed: **"For I am not ashamed of the Gospel of Christ: for it is the power of God unto salvation...for THEREIN is the Righteousness of God revealed..."** (Rom. 1:16,17). Additional support to the fact that none can savingly know God prior to hearing and believing the Gospel of God, may be found in the following passage of Scripture where Paul was thanking God for the Colossians since he heard of their faith in Christ Jesus, and **"For the hope which is laid up for you in heaven, whereof ye heard before IN THE WORD OF THE TRUTH OF THE GOSPEL; Which is come unto you, as it is in all the world; and bringeth forth fruit, as it doth also in you, SINCE THE DAY YE HEARD OF IT, and KNEW THE GRACE OF GOD IN TRUTH"** (Col. 1:5,6). The only place these Colossians heard of the hope of heaven was the Gospel and the only time the evidence of its fruit was manifest was *since* the day they heard it and not *prior* to that glorious day when they heard of and knew the God of grace IN TRUTH. The only place where you will hear of the grace of God *in truth* is the Gospel of God. Only then can a person truly believe in the God of all grace. Trusting in Christ is inextricably connected with the Gospel of Christ. **Therefore, without the hearing, understanding and believing of the GOSPEL OF CHRIST, there can be no true trusting in the CHRIST OF THE GOSPEL.** In other words and in accord with Peter's statement in 1 Peter 1:23, none can possibly be born again of the incorruptible Seed of God unless they have heard the Gospel, understood it and believed it (see 1 Pet. 1:25).

There is no new birth without the Gospel. It is the most central, vital and core element to the creation of a new creature in Christ and without it there is simply no life (2 Tim. 1:10). Many may claim to trust in Christ but, as we have seen in Ephesians 1:13 and Colossians 1:5,6, the Holy Word of God declares that none **can** trust in Him for they do not, and cannot, know Him unless they have, **by His will** and **by His Gospel,** been born again. Listen to the language of the apostle Paul as he reminds the Corinthians as to how they have come to be born again and made new creatures in Christ: **"...in Christ Jesus I have begotten you THROUGH**

THE GOSPEL" (1 Cor. 4:15). The word *'begotten'* here means *'to procreate, to regenerate, to bear, be born, bring forth, conceive, make, spring'*. The word *'begotten'* is used metaphorically in this verse for *'one who by means of preaching the Gospel becomes the human instrument in the impartation of spiritual life'* (see also Philemon 10). This is yet another occasion in Scripture where we see man's spiritual birth inseparably connected with the Gospel of God. **As he is no Christian that is without the Holy Spirit** (Rom. 8:9)**, so, too, there can be no new birth without the Seed of the Gospel of God by which a man can be cleansed and sanctified.** There can be no new creature without the Gospel of God and there can be no Bible-based trust in Christ the Savior unless the eternal Gospel has been received by means of hearing and understanding it, for the True Christ is revealed and found only in the Gospel (Rom. 1:16,17). The only time a man will hear of the True Christ is when he hears the True Gospel. Anything before that is a false gospel and a counterfeit christ. **The Gospel is the vehicle in which God has placed the eternal and essential truths concerning His Son, Jesus Christ.**

Scripture literally teaches that to be born again is to be **BORN OF THE GOSPEL!** To actually be given birth to by the Gospel Message applied to the heart by God's Holy Spirit. **There is no new birth before it or without it and none can be born of God whilst in ignorance of His Gospel.** The Gospel Message is the very Seed of God wherein eternal life is encased. The Word of Truth by which a man is sanctified (made holy) is the Gospel of Christ. No one can rightly say they have been born again, born of God, unless they have heard, understood and believed the Word of God, His Gospel, which is **the Seed that must be sown** in their hearts that there might be life. Unless they have had that Seed of God sown in hearts prepared by God to receive it, it will not take root and they cannot bear good fruit. In the parable of the sower, the Lord Jesus identifies the Seed sown by the sower as the Word of God: **"Now the parable is this: THE SEED IS THE WORD OF GOD"** (Lk. 8:11; see also Mk. 4:14; Matt. 13:19). Christ explained in Matthew's record of the parable: **"But he that RECEIVED seed into the good ground is he** *that HEARETH the Word, and UNDERSTANDETH it; which also beareth fruit..."* (Matt. 13:23). We see then that **receiving the seed** into good ground is defined as **hearing the Word and understanding it**. The only time there can be any evidence of the fruit of the Gospel is AFTER it is sown, or preached, and received into good ground, or **heard and understood** (see also Col. 1:6).

In light of this, it stands to biblical reason that if there is no hearing of the Gospel, if that incorruptible Seed of God is not sown into good ground, that is, into a heart prepared by God to receive it, **there can be no new creature**. Imagine someone expecting a plant to pop up out of the ground *before* the seed has been sown! First must come the seed *then* the life. **If there is no seed there is no life and if there is no life then there can be no evidence of regeneration.** No amount of will power could ever be the catalyst for plant life, so, too, no amount of religious traditionalism or sincere religious zeal or will power or flowery sentiment or experiences or tears of remorse can bring about spiritual life. **THERE MUST BE A SEED** and it **must** be God's Seed, **the Gospel**, for there is no other seed which can produce a new creature in Christ! It must be noted that simply because there has been seed sown, that is no guarantee that it will bear fruit. Just as there is no fruit from the seed which is scattered upon a rock, where there is hearing but no understanding of what is heard, there can likewise be **no new birth** according to Scripture, for if there is no understanding, no comprehension, there can be no believing, in the biblical sense of the word, and therefore no genuine trusting. Again, what the Bible calls true trusting in Christ can only occur AFTER the Gospel is heard and believed (see Eph. 1:13). Understanding, and therefore believing from the heart, is a sure sign that the person is no longer dead to God and His glorious Message, but that God, by His wonderous grace, has made that person alive to Him. The Light of the glorious Gospel has shone upon him that understands, savingly, and the Gospel is no longer hid from him (see 2 Cor. 4:3,4).

Again, James tells us that the born again person is one who is made so by the immutable WILL OF GOD with the

Gospel Message, by the preaching of it, which is the means God has chosen to make His Message heard (see 1 Cor. 1:21 & Jas. 1:18). The passage where 1 Corinthians 1:21 is from shows that that preaching is the preaching of the Cross of Christ (see 1 Cor. 1:17-24), which lies at the heart of the Gospel Message. **Man is not born again of his own will and in his own way, but by God's will and by God's Way: the Gospel.** Man is not born again out of his own sincerity or because of any conviction that a certain religious experience he once had, or is having, came from God. **SINCERITY IS NOT THE SEED and therefore no amount of it can bring forth a new creature in Christ, for this is wholly the domain of the True Seed of Christ: His Gospel. Sincerity of belief is not the evidence, proof or qualifier for salvation.** Everyone believes something and most are very sincere in their beliefs, but **it is WHAT a man believes that is the central issue and not how sincerely he believes it. Sincerity is not the key to freedom, it is the TRUTH of God which makes a man free:** *"And ye shall know the Truth, and the Truth shall make you free"* (Jn. 8:32). It is vital for all to realise that **<u>GODLY SINCERITY IS ALWAYS ACCOMPANIED BY GOD'S TRUTH.</u>** Joshua 24:14 says: *"Now therefore fear the Lord, and serve Him in SINCERITY and in TRUTH: and put away the gods which your fathers served on the other side of the flood, and in Egypt; and serve ye the Lord"* (see also 1 Cor. 5:8; 2 Cor. 1:12; 2;17). **Sincerity without Truth always leads to false gods and false religions.** Man is not born again through some mystical experience or practice, real or imagined, no matter how wonderful it may make him feel or how *'spiritual'*. Man is not born again through anything which is not tangible. **He is not born again by means of anything outside of the Gospel.** Man is born again through hearing and understanding the Word of God, which is His Gospel. This is what the Scriptures teach. It is important to note that a man can, over a period of time, hear the Gospel and gradually reach the point where he understands and believes it, but **the man is not born again <u>during</u> this period** but only AFTER he has fully understood and believed the Gospel: *"In Whom (Jesus) ye* *also trusted, AFTER that ye heard the Word of Truth, the GOSPEL of your salvation: in Whom also AFTER ye believed, ye were sealed with that Holy Spirit of promise"* (Eph. 1:13). We see then that **NONE** can be sealed with that Holy Spirit of promise *before* they have believed the glorious Gospel, and **NONE** can trust in Christ *before* they have heard His Mighty Gospel. In John 6:44, the Lord Jesus says that *"No man can come unto Me, except the Father which hath sent Me DRAW him..."*(see also Jer. 31:3). This *drawing* is done by their being taught of God: *"...And they shall be all taught of God. Every man therefore that hath heard, and hath LEARNED of the Father, cometh unto Me"* (Jn.6:45). Just as a net full of fish being drawn to shore or into the boat is not **in** the boat or **on** the shore until the drawing is completed, so, too, none can be said to be **in Christ** whilst the drawing (*dragging*) is taking place but only **after** the process is completed. The new birth of any man is by the will of God and the means He uses for each and every man's spiritual birth does not differ. It is always by His Mighty and Glorious Message which is His Gospel: *"For I am not ashamed of the Gospel of Christ: for IT IS THE POWER OF GOD UNTO SALVATION to everyone THAT BELIEVETH..."* (Rom. 1:16; see also Psa. 19:7).

Reference was made earlier to those people who claim to be Christians and yet have never heard the true Gospel, who basically judge themselves saved based on their sincerity, regardless of whether or not they now believe the Gospel, and to those who claim to believe the Gospel but insist they were saved long before they ever heard it. The only consistency in such warped and unscriptural views as these is their **inconsistency** with what the Scriptures teach. We have just learned what the Scriptures clearly say concerning being born again: precisely how and when a man is made a new creature in Christ. Yet most who profess to believe in Christ remain in a dead state without God, for in saying that they were born again before they heard the Gospel, **they deny the very Gospel itself and its exclusivity of power to save,** without which no man can be born again. No person can rightly say they **fully** believe

God's Message if they insist that they were born again **before actually hearing it**, for the Message itself condemns all those who do not believe it, including all those who say they were born again without it. If God has said that no man can be born again unless it is by His incorruptible Seed, i.e. The Gospel, and a man says that he was born again without having heard this Gospel, or having a limited understanding of it, or even agreeing with most but not all of it, it is clear that the man stands deluded; that he contravenes the Word of God; that he calls God a liar and that he has embraced a false gospel, which brings with it a false sense of security and a counterfeit salvation. **Any gospel that speaks peace to you and assures you that you were saved before you ever heard it, is a false gospel which has not come to you from God but from a lying spirit.** If the power of God *unto salvation* is identified by Scripture as the Gospel (Rom.1:16) and the preaching of the Cross (1Cor.1:18), then by what *power*, it may be well asked, were those *'saved'* who claim to have been saved without the Gospel? **Anyone who claims that they were saved before they heard the Gospel is really saying that they were saved without the power of God!!** The children of delusion who say they were saved before hearing the Gospel are saying that for a certain period, at least, in their lives they were saved outside of hearing and understanding the Gospel Message, without which no man can be saved. **If receiving the Gospel, which is the power of God unto salvation, consists of hearing and understanding it, how can any rightly say they were saved by the power of God before they ever heard and understood the Gospel of God?**

It is made abundantly clear in the words of the Lord Jesus Christ in the following Scripture that there is no life prior to, or without, the Gospel of Christ. Immediately after commanding His disciples to go into all the world and preach the Gospel to every creature, Christ said: *"He that believeth* (the Gospel) *and is baptized shall be saved; but he that believeth not* (the Gospel) *shall be damned"* (Mk. 16:16). In light of these words by the Son of God, how can any man rightly say he is born again unless he has had that incorruptible Gospel Seed of God sown in his heart? How can any man be in a saved state before believing the Gospel, when Christ has plainly stated here that **any who do not believe the Gospel are in a damned state! The number one identifying principle as to whether a man is saved or not is: DOES HE BELIEVE THE GOSPEL!** If so, then he is saved. If not, or he has not heard the Gospel, he is lost. Nothing could be simpler for our minds to grasp and **by which we can scripturally draw the line between saved and lost**. Not only will those who do not believe the Gospel be damned if they remain in this state, but according to Christ's words found in John 3:18, they already stand condemned: **"He that believeth on Him is not condemned: but he that believeth not is condemned already, because he hath not believed in the name of the only begotten Son of God."** *Believing in the name* of Christ is equivalent to believing the Gospel, for His name speaks of His Person and Work, which is what the Gospel is all about (see Matt. 1:21). I am sure this is all made abundantly clear, even to the simplest mind, and needs no scholarly intellect or Bible college degree to grasp what is being said here. However, I believe it *would* require a scholarly mind and a professorial degree to make any sense of the empty and nonsensical argument held to by those who profess to have been born again without having heard and understood the Gospel.

      Multitudes of people place unflinching trust in their many and varied religious experiences, in their sincerity, in their faith, in their religious leaders and in what they call their *'love for God,'* not to mention all the *'answers to prayer'* they have witnessed in their lives and see all this as irrefutable evidence that God had saved them long before they ever heard the Gospel. As one man has wisely stated, *"Everyone thinks they are saved, before they are saved, until they are saved."* (W.P.) It must be added at this point that most professing christians have never been presented with the True Gospel but a phony one which cannot save. And, it must also be said that the bulk of men who have set themselves up as 'christian' ministers do not *knowingly* set out to deceive their listeners with a false gospel, but are just as deceived by the counterfeit gospel they proclaim as their listeners are.

Nevertheless, Christ states: **"Let them alone: they be blind leaders of the blind. And if the blind lead the blind, both shall fall into the ditch"** (Matt. 15:14). **They are false teachers whose message offers no true salvation and speaks of another jesus** (see 2 Cor. 11:13-15). Another of the key factors which convinces people they are truly saved and have found the true God, is the moral reformation that they have experienced since the time of their perceived conversion, in their turning away from immorality to morality. They see the evidence of a moral life accompanying their beliefs about God, and count it as godliness. **This is a fatal error and one which deceives the whole world.** If all that *godliness* means is a high level of morality, then we must count Mormons, among others, as saved people. The reason most professing christians would scoff at this is because they know full well that, despite the high level of morality in the lives of Mormons, their various doctrines about Who Christ is and what Christ has done show conclusively that they do not hold to the doctrine of Christ, and that they are even in disagreement with some of the most basic tenets of the Christian Faith.

Many see how *'lovely'* and *'nice'* and *'christian'* their friends are who attend the same church as they do, and promptly judge them all saved. Generally, most believe that they began their Christian lives in ignorance of most of what the Bible teaches, but claim to have *believed enough* to convince themselves that they definitely were converted on such and such a day. They also subscribe to the popular notion that *'it really doesn't matter what you believe, but how you live is what is really important.'* Most believe that all one needs to believe at the beginning of their Christian life, and whilst in their infant state as Christians, is that Christ died for sinners. Some even quote 1 Corinthians 15:3,4 and say that all one needs to believe to be saved is the death, burial and resurrection of Christ. If this were true, then every Roman Catholic and Mormon out there would have to be considered as truly saved people, because they, too, all believe that Christ died for sinners. What these *simplifiers* of the Gospel—what they really are is minimizers—do not realize, is that the Scriptures just mentioned, which they often refer to, include one very important qualifier and that is that a Christian believes in the death, burial and resurrection of Christ **ACCORDING TO THE SCRIPTURES!** *"For I delivered unto you first of all that which I also received, how that Christ died for our sins ACCORDING TO THE SCRIPTURES: And that He was buried, and that He rose again the third day ACCORDING TO THE SCRIPTURES"* (1 Cor. 15:3,4). The death, burial and resurrection of Christ, as mere historic events, is NOT what the Bible teaches. What it does teach is the death, burial and resurrection of Christ **ACCORDING TO THE SCRIPTURES** and not according to anything or anyone else. The *Scriptures* spoken of here is a reference to the Old Testament, whose types and sacrifices all pointed to the coming Messiah, and to the prophecies made regarding the Messiah and what He would do.

Many 'teachers' in Protestant denominations today say that a man must believe the Gospel, but then fail to identify and distinguish that Gospel from all others. **Rarely do they ever say that a person who names the name of Christ, yet abides not in the doctrine of Christ, is lost.** And most of their followers simply presume that they know the Gospel, when all they know are a few historical facts about what happened to the Messiah and a couple of things they *'haven't worked out yet'*. Allow me to make it quite clear that **the Gospel is NOT about believing in what HAPPENED TO the Messiah, but is about KNOWING and believing Who the Messiah IS by what the Messiah DID to save His people from their sins.** Christ said: *"And this is life eternal, that they might KNOW Thee the only true God, and Jesus Christ, Whom Thou hast sent"* (Jn.17:3). God says: *"...Let not the wise man glory in his wisdom, neither let the mighty man glory in his might, let not the rich man glory in his riches: But let him that glorieth glory in this, THAT HE UNDERSTANDETH AND KNOWETH ME..."* (Jer. 9:23,24). Many highly regarded Reformed ministers, including many *'great'* teachers of the past with lofty reputations such as Charles Spurgeon, taught that after one's initial conversion all christians end up taking one theological path or the other. Some choose to go down the Arminian path and others the Calvinistic path, but these ministers, including Spurgeon, insist both these paths lead to the same God! This, in spite of the fact that Spurgeon readily recognized and labelled the Arminian gospel as *another gospel*! **If both 'paths' lead to the same God, they then must of necessity come from the same God but seeing that the two belief systems of Arminianism and Calvinism are so obviously and diametrically opposed, this simply could not be.** What Spurgeon was saying, and what those ministers who, it must be said, so blindly follow in his footsteps are saying, is that whether one believes that Christ died for everyone or exclusively for the elect, both *'types of believer'* are headed for the same heaven and *'essentially'* believe the same Gospel. It does not matter, according to these people, who exactly Christ's precious blood was shed for or what you believe Christ accomplished by His death. *"This is not necessary in knowing the True Christ and trusting in His accomplishments,"* they say, *"as long as you believe in the Messiah who died on a cross for sins, in particular your sins, then you are a Christian, God is in His heaven and all is well with the world."* But, friend, all is not well, for such a view is at odds with the Scriptures, which state emphatically that **if it is not the Gospel Message OF Christ, and ABOUT Christ, which you believe in your heart and hold to with every fibre of your being, you cannot be one who has been born of God's will through the Gospel, who truly trusts IN Christ**, but you remain dead in your sins and hold to the teachings of mere men. You may well be religious and extremely zealous in that religion, but your zeal is not according to knowledge, **the knowledge of God's Eternal Gospel,** without which no man can be born again. **The 'reasoning' which these ministers have adopted allows for a man's gospel to be riddled with error and still provide him with salvation.** In fact, two men can believe in totally opposing views about what the Gospel is, **Who Christ is and what He has done**, and still be labelled as saved *'believers of the Gospel'* by most ministers today. If they are right, where do we draw the line? How wrong would a person have to be to disqualify them from being a true believer? Where are the Scriptures that support such reasoning and what then would the Gospel actually be?

saved paled into insignificance when faced with the true Gospel of God. Granted, there was some minor trepidation in looking at my religious past with all of its experiences and *'good deeds'* and *'glorious moments'* in prayer and Bible studies etc., and coming to terms with the fact that I was to turn my back on it all and count it as dung just as the apostle Paul did his religious past before hearing and believing the Gospel (see Phil. 3). But by the mighty grace of God and His Great Gospel, which I could not, cannot and never will be able to deny, I let go of all that was and all that I was and thought myself to be before I heard and understood the True Gospel, which introduced me to the True Christ. I promptly counted the false gospels and false christs I had once believed in as rubbish for the excellency of the knowledge of THE Lord Jesus Christ, as revealed to me in the Gospel of God.

As was mentioned earlier, the most popular view about conversion and by which most judge themselves to be born again, is the evidence of a moral change in one's life, a new found desire to know the things of God and a basic belief in Christ's death, burial and resurrection. Most believe that as babes in Christ we know very little of the doctrine of Christ. At worst, such a view as this dispenses with the value and necessity of sound doctrinal knowledge being the primary evidence of a converted life, and at best it is reduced to something which is an added extra to one's religious life but not an essential and vital ingredient, at least not at the outset. Every woman knows that one cannot make an omelette without eggs. You cannot add the eggs after the filling or while one is in the midst of consuming it. The eggs must be added at the outset or you simply end up with an untidy mess rather than a finely and properly prepared omelette, which would be readily recognized and rightly called an omelette. So, too, one cannot have a true belief in Christ, and be rightly called a Christian, if one does not have the doctrine of Christ: **"Whosoever transgresseth, and abideth not in the doctrine of Christ, hath not God..."** (2 Jn. 9). The word *'abideth'* here not only means *'to stay or remain in a place'* but also *'to be present'* or *'stand'*. One cannot have God if one does not abide in the Gospel of God, if one does not stand in, and with, His doctrine. *"To be and* *remain united with Him, one with Him in heart, mind and will."* **In other words, to be in agreement with His Testimony, His Doctrine, His Gospel.** While you stand outside of that Gospel or are ignorant of it, you are one who does not have God. It is important to note the connection which Scripture makes between sound doctrine and the Gospel. Paul said that the Christian is to be wary of anything **"...*that is contrary to SOUND DOCTRINE: According to the glorious GOSPEL of the blessed God...*"** (1 Tim. 1:10,11; see also 2 Tim. 4:2-4; Titus 1:9). (See the author's booklet 'God Loves Doctrine')

Most subscribe to the well-worn teaching that, as babes in Christ, we know little of Christ and our views are sprinkled with much error, but as we grow and mature we eventually *come into the right knowledge* of Him and are corrected and instructed by Scripture as we go along and become adults in Christ. The erroneous doctrines are replaced by *truer* doctrines. *But through even our doctrinally darkest days we were Christians,* they insist. This all sounds so convincing and logical that no wonder those who believe it have no problem with such 'reasoning'. Most have never heard anything different from this and because it matches with most other experiences in life where man starts off in relative ignorance or having little knowledge of a matter, he later grows and becomes more knowledgeable and mature in what he practices or believes. Yet, the meaning of the key phrase *'babe'* in Christ, often used in this line of reasoning as a defense for the religionists' ignorant, but to their minds, nonetheless saved state, is totally misrepresented and misunderstood and is completely at odds with the fact that every true believer *from the beginning* of their Christian lives to final glory **knows** the doctrine of Christ and abides in it. 2 John 9 shows clearly that it could not be otherwise, and that **all who are not present, or stand not, in Christ's doctrine have not God**. This could never be said of a true believer, for whether he is a young Christian or one who has been in the faith for many years, he abides in the doctrine of Christ and no other. If he is in Christ he stands with Christ's doctrine for it is CHRIST'S Voice which he has heard and does follow and not that of a stranger (Jn. 10:4,5,27).

It must be asked, *'How does one get to be a babe in Christ? What is it to be a babe in Christ? What makes the difference between one who is a religious, professing christian yet dead in his sins, and one who is a babe in Christ? How ignorant can one be and yet still be biblically referred to as a babe in Christ?'* It might also be asked, *'Where on earth did man ever get the idea that to be a babe in Christ meant that one was ignorant of the doctrine of Christ?'* In light of 2 John 9 where it is stated that if one does not abide in the doctrine of Christ one does not have God, being a babe in Christ could not be a proper definition of one who is ignorant of the doctrine of Christ, that is, Who Christ is, what Christ has done and for whom He has done it. **He could not possibly be ignorant of the Gospel, for he has been born of the Gospel! Remember, a babe in Christ is just as much a creature born again, born of God's Seed, the Gospel, as one who is mature in Christ.** If you are in Christ you are in Christ and your life is hid with Him in God (Col. 3:3). If you are in Christ you abide in His doctrine and have God, if not, if you do not abide in the doctrine of Christ, you cannot be in Christ and therefore you simply cannot have God. To be a babe in Christ never has referred to, and never could be a description of, one who is ignorant of the Person and Work of Christ, for this would fly in the face of the Bible's definition of what a truly born again new creature in Christ is: one who believes the Gospel.

The term *'babe'* in the New Testament which refers to those *'babes in Christ'* is found in Hebrews 5:13: **"For every one that useth milk is unskilful in the word of righteousness: for he is a babe"** (see also 1 Cor. 3:1 ff.). It is important to note firstly that who the writer here refers to as *'babes'* are Christians. All are agreed that the writer has addressed his Epistle to Hebrew converts to Christianity and that there is nothing in the Epistle which would suggest otherwise. That means that they are all people who have been born again, born of that Holy Seed: the Gospel of Jesus Christ. It means that they have heard the Gospel and have understood it so as to give evidence that they are new creatures in Christ. *"The Gospel had been preached and 'confirmed' unto them"* (Heb. 2:1-3). They are considered brethren throughout the Epistle (Heb. 3:1,12; 10:19; 13:22) and if brethren, then they must be believers. Believers in what? Why, the Gospel of course! How do I know? **Because every born again believer is born of the incorruptible Seed of God: the Gospel** (1 Pet. 1:23-25). EVERYONE THAT IS SAVED IS A BELIEVER IN THE GOSPEL (Mk. 16:16). Again, before hearing and understanding the Gospel, no one can rightly consider themselves a new creature in Christ, **for the primary characteristic feature of a new creature in Christ is that he believes the Gospel**. It is the principle form of judging a man saved, otherwise why would the Lord Jesus have stated in Mark 16 that a man is saved based on whether or not he believes the Gospel? The works of a man are important but they are not what is identified by Christ as THE identifying characteristic of a true believer. **Just as faith without works is dead so, too, works without THE Faith of Christ is just as dead.**

The word *'unskilful'* in Hebrews 5:13 means *'inexperienced,' 'ignorant'.* Yet it cannot mean ignorance of the Gospel in the sense that they had not heard it and therefore did not believe it, for then one could become born of the Gospel without knowledge of that Gospel! It would mean that Christ was wrong when He taught that the Seed, His Word that was sown into the good ground, needed to be heard and understood before it could bring forth fruit (see Matt. 13:23). It would run contrary to the whole flow of Scripture which states quite clearly that a Christian is one who is saved and believes the Gospel, and, that one who is ignorant of that Gospel, and to whom that Gospel is hid, or who simply does not believe it, is damned (see Mk. 16:16 & 2 Cor. 4:3). It does not mean that they are without knowledge of the Gospel. *"Now the Hebrews are not here said to be ignorant of or utterly without the Word of Righteousness* (the Gospel of Grace), *but 'unskilful' or 'inexperienced' in the use of it. They had failed to improve it to its proper end."* Whereas by now they should have been teachers (v.12) they remained infants in their knowledge of the Gospel, yet not in absolute ignorance of it. **They did not know the Gospel as intimately as those who feed on strong meat** (v.14). It does not mean that they are not Christians *"...but that they* *had not the experience or skill requisite to enable them to understand* (or proclaim) *the higher mysteries of the Christian religion. They understand the great system only as a child may."* **But understand it they do.** There is a vast difference between understanding something, albeit in its basic form, and being altogether ignorant of it *or even part of it.* According to Hebrews 5:12, these believers had been Christians long enough to now be teachers but instead, though knowing the basics of the Gospel, they were not as learned in the deeper mysteries of the Gospel Message and could not articulate it as well as they should have been able to by this time. *"It was not that they had lost, absolutely, their knowledge of Divine Truth, but they had failed to lay it to heart, and live in the power of it."* Hebrews 5:12 tell us that these babes needed to be taught again of **"...the first principles of the oracles of God..."** *"...They needed to be reminded of the ways in which the* (Old Testament) *tabernacle, its services, priesthood, etc., all typified the work of Christ (see Heb. 2:17; 3:3; 4:14; 5:4-10; 6:19,20). Perhaps they also needed to be reminded of the promises they had received in the Old Testament; not only the greatness and the preciousness of the promises (see Heb. 1:5,13; 2:11,12; 8:8-12; 10:9,10; 11:40), but also the certainty with which they would be fulfilled (see Heb. 6:13-19; 7:21; 8:6; 9:11; 10:12-14, 19-22; 12:25; 13:8)* (C.A.). Hebrews 6:1 tells us that these *babes* were encouraged to **"...go on unto perfection and not laying again the foundation of repentance from dead works..."** The *dead works* here is a reference to the ceremonial laws of the Old Testament, of which the babe in Christ had obviously already repented. **Doubtless, the writer to the Hebrews would not have said of these that they should by now be teachers who were not in fact Christians to begin with.** He would not have said **"For when for the time ye ought to be teachers..."** (Heb. 5:12), but rather, *"For when for the time ye ought to be Christians..."* Also, the author of the Epistle would not have referred to these babes as *unskilful* in the Word of Righteousness, but rather absolutely unfamiliar with it, were they not believers to begin with.

The Scriptures we have already seen in this study show us plainly that to be a babe in Christ one must have been born of God's incorruptible Seed: His Gospel. 1 Peter tells us that the new creature in Christ is **born again by the Word of God** (1 Pet. 1:23). *"Therefore if any man be IN CHRIST, he is a new creature..."* (2 Cor. 5:17). One is either *in Christ,* or *of the world*, according to the Scriptures (see Jn. 17:14,21). And, if one is said to be **in Christ** then he must be in a saved state, and, if in a saved state then he must be a believer of the Gospel of Christ. According to the Bible, no babe in Christ is ignorant of that Christ, for each and every babe in Christ has been born of the Gospel of Christ. None can be properly considered a babe, or baby, in Christ, who has not firstly been born—born of that Seed of God—His Gospel. According to 2 Corinthians 5:17 and 1 Peter 1:23, everyone who is a new creature is born of the Gospel and is said to be in Christ. No one is a babe in Christ who has not received His Seed into good ground, which is to hear and understand His Mighty Gospel (Matt. 13:23). **A babe in Christ has much to learn and is encouraged to grow in his knowledge of God and of Christ** (see Col. 1:10) **and learn in finer detail the intricacies and excellencies of the Gospel Message, but none can be said to be ignorant of that Message, for this new creature has been born of that Message.** He heard it and understood it right from the start! To have faith in God is far more than a mere acknowledgement of His existence and that He is kind and loving and merciful. *"It is faith in God in regard to His existence <u>and</u> perfections, <u>and</u> to His plan of saving men. It includes, therefore, <u>faith in His Message and Messenger,</u> and thus <u>embraces the plan of salvation by the Redeemer."</u>* Just as there can be no natural, physical conception without the seed of man, so, too, there can be no supernatural, spiritual conception without the Seed of God. How can a man produce an offspring without the seed of man? He cannot. It is a physical impossibility. God has set an immutable law on the earth, that without the seed of man there can be no physical offspring from man. God has also set an equally immutable **spiritual** law, which is just as definable and specific and set in concrete as that which He has laid down as an inescapable prerequisite for the physical birth of any man. **No one can be born again, that is, born spiritually, without the Seed of God, which is His Holy Gospel Message.** None can become new creatures in Christ, and therefore be IN Christ, unless it is by means of God's Gospel, unless they have heard and understood the Gospel of Christ. **"But if our Gospel be hid, it is hid to them that are lost"** (2 Cor. 4:3). This Scripture shows clearly that if the Gospel is hidden, that is, if anyone is ignorant of the Gospel, or they simply do not believe it, they are lost. It is as uncomplicated as that. One can have all the religion in the world and be squeaky clean morally and ethically, but if one does not know the Gospel of God, if that Gospel is concealed, the Bible, far from declaring such a person saved, albeit ignorant of the means used to 'save' him, states that he is **LOST** in that ignorance! None can hear the Gospel unless someone is sent to preach that Gospel Message (see Rom. 10:14-16) and none can in turn understand and believe the Gospel message unless it is revealed to them and the Holy Spirit is sent to apply it to their hearts and they are given the gift of Faith to believe it.

A human baby is still a human regardless of the fact that it has yet to mature etc. Spiritually speaking, a Christian baby is not a creature which is simply alive and will gradually and eventually *evolve through accumulation of knowledge into* a new creature in Christ. The only way he could be a baby in Christ is if he is born of Christ. Some may argue, *'yes, but the reference to 'babe' in Hebrews 5:13 does not include 'in Christ'.* True, but as was pointed out earlier, the letter to the Hebrews was written to Hebrew converts to Christianity and so, according to **the context,** the *'babe'* referred to must be speaking of one who is a babe *in Christ.* If that will not satisfy the reader, there is reference made in 1 Corinthians 3:1 to **'babes in Christ'** and these are clearly spoken of as **'brethren'** in the same verse. The Christian baby is a new creature in Christ from birth. **That's the only kind of creature which God's incorruptible Seed gives birth to.** The very fact that he has been born of that Gospel Seed shows he is now **in Christ**. And, if he is in Christ he is **complete** in Christ (Col. 2:10). One cannot say that one was a saved, albeit ignorant, religious person who *'came into'* the knowledge of the doctrine of Christ years after they were initially *converted* whilst submitted to a false gospel, for what would they base their *conversion* on? Nothing less than what any religious person bases their conversion on: *a changed life, a new set of morals* and *a religious viewpoint on life and death*. Ignorance of the Gospel, which is often associated with darkness in the Bible, is not something which the Scriptures teach is synonymous with becoming a Christian. The Christian is not born of darkness or in darkness but he is surrounded and submerged in Light: the Light of the glorious Gospel of Christ! Whilst dead in sin he, just like any man, sat in darkness and loved that darkness and hated light (Jn. 3:19). **"Whereunto He CALLED YOU BY OUR GOSPEL, to the obtaining of the glory of our Lord Jesus Christ"** (2 Thess. 2:14). Here we are told that the believer is unmistakenly **called of God by the Gospel**. In the following verse we learn what the believer is called out from and what he is brought into. Peter said that the Christian is to **"...shew forth the praises of Him Who hath CALLED YOU OUT OF DARKNESS INTO HIS MARVELLOUS LIGHT"** (1 Pet. 2:9; see also Acts 26:18). **When God calls out His chosen ones He always calls them out by His Gospel from darkness to Light.** They do not remain in darkness but are free from its blinding effects (see 2 Cor. 4:4). The Word of God clearly teaches that to savingly receive the Seed of God, one must hear it **AND** understand it. **Ignorance of the Gospel is ignorance of Christ and ignorance of Christ is absolute and conclusive evidence of a state of lostness.** Christ said of them who believe not on Him: **"That the saying of Isaiah the prophet might be fulfilled, which he spake, Lord, who hath believed our report? And to whom hath the arm of the Lord been revealed? Therefore they could not believe, because that Isaiah said again, He hath blinded their eyes, and hardened their heart; that they should not SEE with their eyes, nor UNDERSTAND with their heart, and be CONVERTED..."** (Jn. 12:38-40). Here we see further evidence that *seeing* and *understanding* are inseparably connected with conversion. What is it that Isaiah spoke of when he said **"...who hath believed our report?"** Would it be reading into the Scriptures that which is not there if we were to say that what Isaiah referred to was the Gospel? Hardly. Paul reveals all in Romans 10:16: ***"But they have not all obeyed THE GOSPEL. FOR ISAIAH SAITH, LORD, WHO HATH BELIEVED OUR REPORT?***

Christ **is** the Gospel, and the preaching of the Cross is the core element to Gospel preaching. There is no Gospel without Christ; there is no Gospel without the true preaching of the Cross of Christ which is foolishness to them that perish but to those who believe **it is the power of God** (1 Cor. 1:18). Without Christ and without the Cross, there would not only be no Gospel but NO CHRISTIANS! How could there be if they know nothing of the Messiah sent of God to save His people from their sins, the Person and Work of that Messiah being central to the Gospel Message? Mysticism plays no part in true Christianity. To truly follow Christ and be a spiritual babe in Christ does not in any way suggest ignorance of that Christ but, conversely, it shows that one does know the Person and Work of Christ. This is not to say that a spiritual babe knows all there is to know of Christ (if such a thing were possible), but he does know the Lord enough to show that he has been born of Him for he has heard and understood the Gospel Message wherein Christ and His Righteousness is revealed. Whether one is a babe in Christ or whether one is a mature believer, one is a Christian and one cannot be a Christian without knowing Who Christ is and what Christ has done. **One cannot be ignorant of the Gospel of Christ and rightly claim to know Him and to believe in Him and His Message.** The mature believer, one who feeds on strong meat and not on milk, is one who has learnt much of the Gospel (Heb. 5:14), and can articulate it better than the babe in Christ. But that babe, though ignorant and inexperienced in the deeper mysteries and glories of the full Gospel Message, knows that basic Gospel Message enough to show he has indeed been born of the Seed of God and knows God. One may ask, *"Yes, but what is it to know the Gospel enough to consider oneself saved?"* It is to know the Person and Work of Christ, Who He is and for whom He died. This will be explained in greater detail as we go on.

The Gospel is what **MUST** be believed if one is to show evidence that he is a Christian, born of God. Anyone can show a degree of moral reformation in their lives, but not everyone believes the Gospel. **That is one of the reasons it is foolhardy to judge a person a Christian simply by their outward appearance and conduct.** If one does not believe the Gospel, one is lost (Mk.16:16); if one is ignorant of it, one is lost (2 Cor. 4:3); and if one adds to it or takes away from it knowingly or unknowingly, he is preaching another gospel and shows his lost state (Gal. 1:6-9). Paul made it clear to the Galatians that if any one came to them preaching *anything* different from the Gospel he had told them, they were to consider such people accursed: **"...*if any man preach any other gospel unto you than that ye have received, let him be accursed*"** (Gal. 1:9). Notice, Paul did not say these preachers of a different gospel could actually be fellow Christians but just a little confused or ignorant of what the true Gospel is, for **there is no such creature!** According to Paul's words, if a Christian came to the Galatians he would preach the exact same Gospel that Paul preached, but if any came in Christ's name and preached anything *other than* what Paul had proclaimed, if their gospel differed in any way to any degree with the Gospel Paul had proclaimed, this was to be taken as a **SURE SIGN** that those people were lost and still in darkness, not knowing the Gospel. Those who do not believe the Gospel of Christ demonstrate that they are lost and in need of hearing, understanding and believing God's Message concerning His Son.

It is an enigma to this writer that so many say that the Gospel is something which cannot be defined. They even claim it is something which we *cannot* know! **But if it is something which cannot be defined and that cannot be known, how then can it be preached let alone believed?** Surely if Christ told His people to preach the Gospel (Mk. 16:15), then the Gospel is a message which is known to those who preach it and will be known by those whom God has elected to savingly receive it by way of hearing and understanding it. **If the Gospel is something which is to be preached and heard, then what kind of fool would venture to say that it is something which cannot be understood?** The Bible often warns of false gospels and false teachers (2 Cor. 11:4; 2 Pet. 2:1). How are we to recognise the false gospels and false teachers if we cannot define and know what the True Gospel is? One Reformed minister, no less, has wishfully stated, no doubt with a gleam in his eye, *"If only we could put our finger on what the Gospel is, that would be something."* A more ludicrous, asinine, unscriptural and ungodly statement one would be hard-pressed to find. Let us take such *'reasoning'* to its logical conclusion: If the Gospel is something which cannot be defined, then it must also of necessity be impossible to preach. And, if the Gospel cannot be preached, then how can any man believe it? **A message which cannot be defined cannot be preached.** A message which cannot be preached, and therefore heard, cannot be understood and believed in. How then can an indefinable and unpreachable message possibly be believed in!! The Gospel must be believed if any are to be saved, for man is lost without it. If the Gospel is something which **must** be believed in, then it **MUST** be preachable, **IT MUST BE DEFINABLE!** The main reason the whole Bible was given to man was to convey the Message of the Messiah Who would be sent to the earth to be the Savior of His people. That Message is called the Gospel: the Good News of God to His people, **and is to be preached to every creature!** Why would God keep such a Message, which must be believed in if one is to be rightly judged saved, hidden from His own people whom He has elected to hear it, know it and believe it? **You cannot hear, know and believe something which has not and cannot be defined.** The very fact that a Message needed to be given unto men in the first place shows that prior to hearing, knowing and receiving that Message, all men are in a lost state before a Holy God, **for the plan of Redemption is only revealed in that Gospel Message and can therefore only be believed in after that Message has been preached.** To *preach* the Gospel, which is Christ's command to every believer (Mk. 16:15), *is to* define the Gospel. The fact that a Savior needed to be sent into the world shows that man, without that Savior, is in a hopeless, depraved state stumbling around in religious darkness not knowing the True and only Way to salvation, for he has no idea how to get to God because he is ignorant of the way and means. **That way and means are only disclosed in the Gospel.**

It is clear from Scripture that to know God is to believe God, and to believe God is to believe His Gospel which is nothing less than God's Testimony of Who His Son is and what His Son has done in order to save His people from their sins. To believe anything else is to deny God's Testimony. In fact, Scripture says that Christ will come **"In flaming fire taking vengeance on them that KNOW NOT GOD, and that OBEY NOT THE GOSPEL of our Lord Jesus Christ"** (2 Thess. 1:8; see also 2 Thess. 2:10-12). In light of this verse, let the enemies of the cross try and tell us that knowledge of the Gospel of Christ is not necessary to salvation! Knowledge of the Gospel is not a condition which man must meet in order to *'get saved'* but is an identifying fruit of salvation. **To believe anything more or less than what God has stated is necessary to salvation, is a denial of His Gospel.** *"For the time is come that judgement must begin at the house of God: and if it first begin at us, what shall the end be of them that obey not the Gospel of God?"* (1 Pet. 4:17). The reader will be aware that when one denies something, one has an opposing idea, which is one of the principal reasons why that which is being denied is denied in the first place. This is why it is so important to know **God's** Gospel Message, for if one does not know it or overtly denies it, one is literally rejecting what **God** has stated is **the essential** to saving faith, and one will be seeking salvation in some other way. In essence, God is saying by His Gospel: *"This is My Son, this is what He has done and any denial of My Words is a denial of Him Whom I have sent and declared to be the Savior of His people."* There is only one Faith which believes the True Gospel and that faith is the one which is given unto men by God. Any faith which does not believe God's Message **in its entirety** is a faith which is not the one which God hands out freely by His Sovereign will and grace, but is one which was born in the deceived heart of man or comes from the wicked and subtle mind of Satan. Man has adorned his multitude of false religious beliefs with a plethora of good deeds and charitable self-sacrificing works, but it is to no avail for the faith which originates within man is not the faith that does, or can, believe in God's Gospel. One cannot be born again by corruptible seed or by hearing and believing false teachings. **No one was ever born again, made a new creature in Christ, by believing in a false gospel.** Christ has said *"And ye shall know the Truth, and the Truth shall make you free"* (Jn. 8:32; see also Gal. 3:1; Col. 1:5,6). That Truth is the Word of the Gospel of Christ Jesus. A false gospel is anything which adds to or takes away from God's only Gospel. So then, if you at the start of your so-called christian life believed in anything more or less than God's True Gospel, you were not saved and if you do not believe this and do not believe in His Gospel now, you are still unsaved. Belief in anything but the True Gospel as THE Gospel is a sure sign of lostness!

Pray tell, how can anything incorruptible come from that which is corruptible? How can anything corruptible be pleasing to God? How can anything not of Him or by Him be pleasing to Him? **How can anyone be born again by believing in a false gospel?** No sane person could or would want to argue against such a rationale. How then can the view be biblically vindicated that a person can become a converted Christian, born again of God, a product of His Word, **before** that Word has ever come to them and unless they hear and believe and understand God's Holy Gospel, which is the very means a person is converted by! The following terms are synonymous and they cannot be separated: **born again, born of God, born from above, born of incorruptible Seed, born of the Truth, born of the Gospel**. They all mean the same thing. The seed of dogs gives birth to dogs; the seed of cats gives birth to cats; the seed of sheep gives birth to other sheep and, my friends, take in the profundity of it all if you will: THE SEED OF GOD, WHICH IS HIS GOSPEL, IS THE **ONLY** THING WHICH WILL GIVE BIRTH TO A NEW CREATURE IN CHRIST!! Christ said, *"...that which is born of the Spirit is spirit"* (Jn. 3:6; see also Jn. 4:23,24) . No new creature in Christ can spring from anything else or anywhere else, other than the Holy Gospel of God. **The Gospel is not something you grow into, it is something you are born out of!** It is not something you walk *to,* it is that which you come *from*. You don't *end* at the Gospel, you *start with* the Gospel! Just like a baby does not *eventually* come to meet its mother weeks, months or years after its birth, but is present with her at the point of birth so, too, the babe in Christ is present at its moment of birth with the one who gave birth to it: the GOSPEL. Everyone who was ever born physically into this world had their mother present with them at the time of birth and everyone who has been born again **spiritually** was born in the presence of the Gospel. **No one is born without their mother and no one is born again without the Gospel.** No mother no baby; no Gospel no Christian!

And so we come to the life and death issue of **what exactly the Gospel is**. What is it that must be believed in if one is to show evidence that one is saved, and what is it that if one does not believe it, one gives evidence that one is in a lost state, regardless of how moral and upright a person one might be? The following will be a brief explanation of what the Gospel is. For a more detailed definition, please see my booklets: 'God's Only Gospel', 'God's Only Jesus' and 'Who Are The lost?'

Firstly, Jesus Christ was sent by God the Father to this earth to save His people from their sins (Lk. 1:77 & Gal. 4:4,5). A people who were dead in their sins and dead to God: **"And you hath He quickened, who were dead in trespasses and sins"** (Eph. 2:1). A people who could not and would not come to God, God's Way: **"There is none that understandeth, there is none that seeketh after God"** (see Rom. 3:10-12). A people who went about according to their fallen nature, *doing what was right in their eyes*, trying to establish a righteousness of their own in the hope of pleasing a Just and Holy God and becoming acceptable, by their own efforts, in His sight. This may sound like a noble endeavor but it is abomination in the sight of God, for no man is righteous or can become righteous in and of himself before the Holy God (see Rom. 3:20; Gal. 3:11). As we shall see, **it is not by man's efforts at obedience that he is saved but wholly by the obedience of Christ alone.** Man, by nature, as he is described in Rom. 3:10-12 is ignorant of and not submitted to God's Gospel Message which is **salvation, from beginning to final glory, conditioned on Christ alone**. The apostle Paul prayed for the salvation of those people who had a zeal for God but not according to knowledge. **What knowledge?** The knowledge of Christ's Righteousness; of **God's Way** to salvation (see Rom. 10:1-4). Man can have all the religious zeal in the world; he can busy himself with religious deeds and service all he likes, but if that zeal is not according to the knowledge of the Gospel, it is just a manifestation of his cursed state and what he perceives to be service to God is nothing but dead works and a stumbling in the darkness. Paul had earlier said of such people, that they had *"...not attained to the law of righteousness. Wherefore? Because they sought it not by faith, but as it were by the works of the law..."* (Rom. 9:31,32) and *"...by the works of the law shall no flesh be justified"* (Gal. 2:16; see also Gal. 3:11). Jesus Christ came to this earth **to redeem** all those whom the Father had given Him: *"As Thou hast given Him power over all flesh, that He should give eternal life to as many as Thou hast given Him"* (Jn. 17:2; see also Jn. 17:6,8,9,14-20). These are they whom God had chosen from before the foundation of the world: *"According as He hath chosen us in Him before the foundation of the world..."* (Eph. 1:4). Jesus Christ came to this earth to live a life of perfect obedience and to bear, or carry away, the sins of His people (Isa. 53:8,11), which were imputed unto Him, or charged to His account, and Whose Righteousness was imputed unto them: *"For He hath made Him to be sin for us, who knew no sin; that we might be made the Righteousness of God in Him"* (2 Cor. 5:21). Jesus Christ came to this earth to fulfill His Father's will by saving all whom the Father had elected from before the foundation of the world. Just as with knowing God and sound doctrine, election and the Gospel are also inseparably connected, according to the Scriptures. Paul knew of the Thessalonians' *"...ELECTION of God. FOR our GOSPEL came not unto you in word only but in power and in the Holy Ghost, and in much assurance..."* (see 1 Thess. 1:4,5; 2:13). According to this, believing the Gospel is a sure evidence that you are elect. All Christ's sheep **will** hear and obey His voice and follow Him and they will never perish, but be preserved in Christ eternally: **"My sheep hear My voice, and I know them, and they follow Me: and I give unto them eternal life; and they shall never perish, neither shall any man pluck them out of My hand"** (Jn. 10:27,28; Col. 3:3; Jude 1). Can you begin to see that the Christian Gospel is a definite message with no room for doubt as to what is meant by it and that belief in any other message professing to be the way to salvation is a sure sign of condemnation. For any other message is a denial of the True Person and Work of Christ and that His triumphant death was actually an **accomplishment** and not merely an attempt at making salvation possible (Heb. 9:11,12). **Your doctrine identifies the god you worship!** All God's people will repent of their sins and turn forever from ever having believed that they could do anything to satisfy God's Justice and be obedient enough to merit God's favor, to gain or maintain salvation, and from the thought that they were ever saved when in this condition (2 Tim. 2:25). The apostle Paul said of all his religion and all that he had done, was and believed in, before hearing and abiding in the doctrine of Christ: **"Yea doubtless, and I count ALL things but loss for the EXCELLENCY OF THE KNOWLEDGE of Christ Jesus my Lord: for whom I have suffered the loss of ALL things, and do count them but DUNG, that I may win Christ, and be found in Him NOT HAVING MINE OWN RIGHTEOUSNESS, which is of the law, but that which is through the faith of Christ, THE RIGHTEOUSNESS WHICH IS OF GOD by faith"** (Phil. 3:8,9).

    This is the Jesus that every Christian believes in. This is the doctrine of Christ which every true believer abides in and this is the Gospel by which every Christian is born again. Everything else is corruptible seed from which springs counterfeit christians and false teachers which look and sound just like true Christians but are in fact wolves in sheep's clothing (Matt. 7:15; see also 24:5,11; 2 Cor. 11:13-15). The Lord Jesus illustrates this in His parable of the wheat and the tares. The parable tells us that wheat has been sown as have tares. While the tares look exactly like wheat, they are plants unsuitable for human consumption and are often fed to cattle. If any tares should get mixed with the wheat at harvest time, the grain is separated and fed to poultry. The most common tare in Israel is known as the Bearded Darnel. Significantly, *"It is a poisonous grass, almost indistinguishable from wheat while the two are growing into blade."* Christ explains that the wheat, which He describes as the *good seed*, is sown by the Son of man (Matt. 13:37). In verse 38 Christ further identifies the good seed and declares in no uncertain way exactly who the tares are symbolical of: **"...the good seed are the children of the Kingdom; but the tares are the children of the wicked one; The enemy that sowed them is the Devil..."** (Matt. 13:38,39). Most in christendom today are under the impression that the *field* where the seed and the tares are sown is the Church. But Christ makes it clear in Matthew 13:38 that the field referred to is the world. Many also falsely believe that both the wheat and the tares are symbolic of Christians. Yet Christ, in His definition, clearly describes the *wheat* as the Christians, who are the children of the Kingdom which God has sown, and the tares as those who are of the Devil which he has sown. The tares shall be burned in the fire and the wheat shall be gathered into the Father's barn (Matt. 13:30,40). **"...Every plant, which My heavenly Father hath not planted, shall be rooted up"** (Matt. 15:13).

Those who claim to be believers and those who claim to have been born again whilst ignorant of Christ's doctrine, have not God and are yet in their sins (Rom. 10:1-4). No matter how much they say they believe in the Gospel, they cannot savingly believe it for they maintain that at a time when they were ignorant of that Gospel they were nonetheless saved. Rather than counting all that preceded the Gospel as rubbish, they count it dear and try to hold onto the Gospel *and* their much loved pre-Gospel experiences and religion. This cannot be done and will not be done by the true believer. You cannot say to Christ *'follow me'*, but you must heed His command to **follow Him** and to forsake and repent of all else. Such people are saying that they and many others were saved without the Gospel, which is equivalent to saying they were physically born without the agency of human seed! They deny that knowledge of the true

Christ, revealed only in the Gospel is essential to knowing Him and being truly saved. They are virtually saying that as long as you hold to the basics, it does not matter what you believe about Christ as long as you are sincere in your love for Him and live a moral life. **But if we do not KNOW Who Christ is and what He has done, how can we say we love Him?** Many simply cannot part with the years of religion and church attendance which they were a part of before hearing God's only Gospel wherein Christ's Righteousness is revealed (Rom. 1:16,17). They still maintain their grasp on a false gospel which can do nothing for them, for *"In that gospel is represented another jesus who cannot save."* (W.R.) Again, claiming to be born again without the Seed of God is like saying one was born without the seed of man! It is ludicrous and is an act of spiritual insanity to make such a statement. This would be like saying that one got to one's destination before one actually arrived! **It simply cannot be done.** One man told me that he was saved before he knew *any* doctrine! **This would be like saying one had passed an examination before one had actually seen the questions.** Many refuse to accept, and therefore do not repent of, the fact that their religious works and beliefs prior to their claim of believing in God's only Gospel, **were dead works and idolatry.** Such a person is lost at this point in time because they are **basing their salvation on something other than God's Gospel**. They have made up their own gospel and follow a god of their own imagination who saves without his word. **The Gospel is not seen as the starting point for these people but merely one of the sign posts along the way.**

Belief of the Truth is a distinguishing feature of every true believer. Speaking to true believers, Paul stated: **"...*God hath from the beginning chosen you to salvation through sanctification of the Spirit and* (through) *BELIEF OF THE TRUTH; whereunto He called you BY OUR GOSPEL, to the obtaining of the glory of our Lord Jesus Christ"** (2 Thess. 2:13,14). However, it is said of those who perish, which includes many professing christians, that they do so **"...*because they RECEIVED NOT THE LOVE OF THE TRUTH, that they might be* *saved...that they all might be DAMNED WHO BELIEVED NOT THE TRUTH..."* (2 Thess. 2:10,12). **Not damned principally because they were immoral but damned because THEY DID NOT BELIEVE, and HAD NOT THE LOVE FOR, the Gospel!** Everyone believes they believe the truth or they would not believe it. But most who believe they have the truth, do not have the love of THE Truth and have instead embraced a lie: *"There is a way that seemeth right unto a man, but the end thereof are the ways of death"* (Prov. 16:25). **Professing believers, that is, those who claim to have been saved prior to hearing and believing in God's Gospel, have redefined God's Gospel by wrenching it apart and making room for false doctrines and various 'spiritual' experiences which made them feel 'spiritual' and 'good inside'. They feel sure that they have the truth and the true God, for these things have combined to convict them of God's existence and of the historical fact that Jesus Christ died on a cross for sinners.** This, coupled with a moral reformation, which incidentally any atheist can experience, is evidence enough for them that what they have is THE Gospel. Millions of lost people today believe that God exists and that Christ died on a cross for sins. Hell is full of people who claimed to have believed in Jesus. Demons believe that there is one God and tremble (Jas. 2:19). Many have walked and do walk this earth today 'calling' on the name of Jesus. Christ said that many worshipped Him in vain (see Matt. 15:9). When asked if few would be saved, Christ answered: *"Strive to enter in at the strait gate: for many, I say unto you, will seek to enter in and shall not be able"* (see Lk. 13:23-27). Christ stated in Matthew 7 that *"NOT EVERY ONE that saith unto Me, Lord, Lord, shall enter into the Kingdom of Heaven..."* One must not believe all who come to them in the name of Christ (Matt.24:5) but all must be tested and every one should examine themselves to see whether they are in THE Faith and whether or not they are being taught the Truth by their leaders (1 Jn. 4:1).

People of every religion experience great changes in their lives, but none except the elect of God ever savingly believe in God's Gospel which reveals the highly significant fact that Christ died for His people **according to the Scriptures** (1 Cor. 15:1-3). Paul the apostle had years of religious duty and moral uprightness which he thought recommended him to God. Imagine how many times **Paul had been under the impression that God was answering his many prayers.** But on learning of Christ and His Righteousness as being the **only Way** to salvation, as revealed in God's glorious Gospel, Paul was made to realize the vanity of his efforts, and was by God's grace made to turn his back on and repent of all his imperfect obedience, vain religiosity and all his *Christless* morality, and count it **DUNG** (see Philippians 3). **This is True biblical repentance: rejecting everything one believed formed any part of, or in anyway contributed to, one's 'salvation' prior to hearing the Gospel.** First comes the seed, *then* comes the life. There is no life prior to the seed. Paul knew that before hearing God's Gospel and while being ignorant of the Righteousness of Christ Imputed (see Rom. 10:1-4), he was a lost man. Not an ignorant but nonetheless saved man, but a **LOST** man.

The Bible states that *"...if our Gospel be hid, it is hid to them that are lost: In whom the god of this world hath blinded the minds of them which believe not, lest the Light of the glorious Gospel of Christ, Who is the Image of God, should shine unto them"* (2 Cor. 4:3,4). Obviously then, if the Gospel is hidden or concealed from a man, if he does not know it and cannot see it, the Bible defines such a person at that point in time to be in a lost state. This does not mean that you cannot *know about* Jesus or that God is the Creator etc., but it does mean that you cannot *savingly* KNOW Him, for He is only revealed in the Gospel. **Salvation knowledge, that which is revealed to the heart of man, is the fruit of the Gospel and the only place from whence it comes.** Without the Gospel you cannot know Him and therefore believe in Him and what He has done to save His people from their sins. Knowing God and believing His Gospel are as one and God will take vengeance *"...on them that KNOW NOT GOD and that OBEY NOT THE GOSPEL of our Lord Jesus Christ"* (2 Thess. 1:8). Before a man hears God's Gospel and believes and trusts in that Gospel, he knows not God and is a lost man and not merely ignorant. **One must know the Gospel; one must believe the Gospel; one must obey the Gospel, if one is to know God and consider oneself saved according to God's Word** (Mk. 16:16 & 2 Thess. 1:8). **Ignorance of Christ** does not amount to some harmless lack of doctrinal knowledge which carries with it no consequences, but **it is a deadly and sure evidence that one is in a lost state**. False christs and false gospels abound. One cannot believe in the True Christ and His Gospel if one does not know Who the True Christ is and what He has done. The Bible always equates ignorance with darkness and lostness. **The Gospel is what has been given to deliver a man from that darkness.**

    What professing christendom has often failed to do over the centuries is to actually identify the Gospel, by defining and distinguishing the terms of God's Gospel from all counterfeits. On the few occasions it has done so, it has presented a false gospel. Basically, 'christian' tradition has it that a man is saved if he believes in the existence of God and that His Son died on a cross for sins. **This is NOT the Gospel. If it was then most people who profess to be Christians would be saved.** The Gospel does not simply teach that Christ died for sins, but that **He died for sins according to the Scriptures**. I cannot emphasize this strongly enough, for it is in the Scriptures, and only in the Scriptures, where one can learn what the Messiah would do in and by His death and who He would do it for. Many believe that they first get born again and *gradually* come to learn of God and what He has done for the sinner as revealed in the Gospel. During this period of *'coming to the knowledge'*, one is seemingly permitted to believe in various and conflicting views of what the Gospel is and what it is that Christ has done, but all are considered saved Christians, for *'they all love God'*. This judgement cannot be made in accordance with God's Word (see 1 Sam. 16:7), but is a judgement which is according to the appearance, which is precisely that form of judgement Christ expressly forbids: **"Judge not according to the appearance, but judge righteous judgement"** (Jn. 7:24). Christ said this, not only so that we would not judge a person *lost* based on their outward appearance and actions, but perhaps more importantly, that we would not judge ourselves or anyone else *saved* **based on our/their outward appearance or reputation!** That's not how we are to recognize a Christian. It is of a certainty that a Christian will perform good works and be charitable and helpful and kind etc., but if this were the principal identifying characteristic of a Christian, then multitudes who do not even believe that Christ Jesus is God, would, based on their character and conduct, be wrongly identified as Christians. An upright life is *one* of the evidences that identifies a Christian, but it is not THE evidence which distinguishes a Christian from any other sincerely dedicated religious person. **The Christian is recognized and identified by what he BELIEVES and not primarily by what he does** (2 Thess. 2:13). Christ describes some in Matthew 7 who went about casting out devils and doing many wonderful works, as those who did iniquity. He says to them He does not know them and sends them into outer darkness. Outwardly these people did appear to be Christians. But if one were to judge them Christians based on their outward appearance and perhaps their reputation for doing good works and casting out demons and prophesying, as no doubt many did, they would have been completely wrong. **They were not Christians.** Yet they called Jesus *'Lord'* and they went about doing things *in His very name*. How more *Christian* could you get? But according to Christ's words, He did not know these people therefore they could not have known Him. What they believed about Jesus showed that it was not THE Jesus Whom they followed, but a counterfeit. Everything that they did outwardly looked good, but it was what they believed inwardly about the Messiah—Who He is and what He had done—which showed that they were not His. They had not been born of His Seed, but out of their own religious delusion.

Many hold to corrupt views as to what the Gospel is, but they do not judge themselves saved or lost mainly by what they believe but how they live. They still consider themselves safe and saved, regardless of how right or wrong their doctrines are, because they *'believe in God'* and have undergone a moral revolution in their lives, or because of family tradition. **Many will not change their beliefs about the Gospel because of a departed loved one who never heard, and therefore never believed, the Gospel unto salvation.** Most who call themselves Christians are familiar with popular terms such as *'grace'*, *'saved by grace alone'*, *'saved by faith'*, *'faith in Christ alone'*, *'He's done it all'* etc., but what do these phrases really mean? Some would be surprised to hear that the Roman Catholic Church often uses the term *'grace'* and even *'saved by grace'*. But even after a brief comparison, it becomes obvious that their interpretation of what the word actually means is at odds with God's definition. To be saved by grace does not mean we are saved by God freely enabling us to meet any conditions for salvation that Christ did not fully meet in His life and death, but it means that God has bestowed salvation upon His people purely by His unmerited favor, based on Christ having met **all** the conditions for our salvation and not on anything that the sinner does. One can see by this, that a proper biblical understanding of Gospel terms is absolutely vital if we are to rightly and savingly believe God's Message. Paul states in Romans 10, in perfect agreement with the fact that one is born again only by the incorruptible Gospel of God, that **"...faith cometh by hearing, and hearing by the Word of God"** (Rom. 10:17). This verse of Scripture is immediately preceded by Paul's mention of the Gospel being preached and obeyed. The faith which comes from God does not come after the hearing of a false gospel, but only comes after God's Gospel is heard. Ephesians 1:13 says that we trust Christ only **AFTER** we have heard this Word of Truth which is the Gospel of our salvation. Those who think that exactly what Christ did on the Cross is just a theological sticking point among *'fellow believers'*, have got it drastically wrong. **WHO one believes Christ died for, reveals exactly what that person believes Jesus did on the Cross.** Far from being just a matter of high theology which can be debated amongst *'brethren'*, this is the heart of the Christian Gospel: **Who is Christ and what did He do?** It is an issue which is dealt with at the start of the believer's life and not during it. Scripture refers to only two things as **'the power of God'**. It says that the Gospel is the power of God unto salvation (Rom. 1:16), and, what many are simply not aware of is that 1 Corinthians 1:18 states: **"For THE PREACHING OF THE CROSS is to them that perish foolishness; but unto us which are saved IT IS THE POWER OF GOD." Who Christ is and what Christ has done is revealed in the Gospel by who Jesus died for on the Cross.** He is not the *potential savior* of every individual, He is **THE Savior** of all for whom He lived and died. He is the Savior that came to save His people from their sins by His atoning death, not a *'wannabe'* savior who could only come and *do* his best to make salvation possible and then *hope* for the best. The name 'JESUS' says it all, for it describes Who He is and what He would do: **"And she shall bring forth a Son, and thou shalt call His name JESUS: FOR He SHALL SAVE HIS PEOPLE FROM THEIR SINS"** (Matt. 1:21; see also Isaiah 53). Those who believe Christ came only to make salvation possible for all, not definite for anybody, need to change the name of their *savior*, for the name JESUS simply does not fit who their god is and what he has done.

If one believes that Christ has died for every individual, then one holds to a salvation conditioned on the sinner and his ultimate decision as to whether he accepts or rejects what has been done. He believes in another jesus and another gospel which cannot save. Such a perverted view of the Person and Work of Christ would mean that many for whom Christ died and went to the Cross on the behalf of, to pay the penalty for their sins, will nevertheless go to hell because THEY did not choose to accept what was done for them. For those who say that it is not important *who* one believes Christ has died for, whether it be every individual or exclusively for the elect, I would ask 'would they call '*Messiah'* that One Who died for the elect? Is *He* the Messiah or is the Messiah the one who died for every individual ever born?' **If there is anything that contributes to, and thereby makes the identification of a person significantly easier, it is what that person has done.** If there were two *jesuses* on two separate crosses on Calvary's Hill, one dying for every individual and the other dying for His elect, which one would they choose? Only one could be the real Savior, the other would be a counterfeit. It cannot be both, for then it must be said of the Messiah that He died on a cross not only for the elect *but also for everyone ever born!* This would mean that the Messiah not only *secured salvation* for His elect but simultaneously *made salvation only possible* for everyone else by the same work! This, needless to say, is a sheer and utter nonsense and shows conclusively that it is vital to know who the real Messiah died for, if one is to believe the True Gospel, for only then can one be said to trust in Him and what He has done. For a deeper study of this, please see this writer's booklet 'Atonement for Whom?' **Man in his natural fallen state simply cannot accept the fact that there is nothing that he can do, or that he is to contribute, in order to gain, or at the least maintain, favor with God.** And so, it is according to man's very nature to seek God and find acceptance with Him by doing some things and abstaining from others. Based on this flawed foundation, the lie has come about that Christ died for every individual, and that the ultimate decision of whether a man goes to heaven or hell is left to man himself. It is not Christ's death that makes the difference but a man's *'free will'*. **In other words, they say it is not God Who makes the difference between saved and lost but the sinner himself.** This runs contrary to such Scriptures as Exodus 11:7: ***"...the Lord doth put a difference between the Egyptians and Israel"*** (see also 1 Cor. 4:7). If I may use such coarse terminology, **God has not prostituted Himself by making Himself available to anyone who will accept Him as long as they agree to His terms. God has PROMISED Himself, in covenant love, to all His elect, His inheritance.** The false gospel teaches that salvation was not obtained or secured by Christ on the Cross for all for whom He died, but that He has only succeeded in making it *possible* for every individual to receive salvation by his own free-will decision. **This changes the very heart of what Atonement is and finds no parallel in the Old Testament types and sacrifices, from which we learn the nature of God-appointed atonement.** The lie of universal atonement in turn does away with the fact that the Bible teaches that man is dead in sin, and replaces it with the satanic lie that man is not dead in sin but merely sin-sick and can, of his own free will, at any time, choose God with a little assistance from God, which they call *'grace'*. The Scripture asks: **"For who maketh thee to differ from another? And what hast thou that thou didst not receive?...."** (1 Cor. 4:7; see also Jn. 3:27). It is God **alone** that makes a saved man to differ from one who is lost. All that a saved man possesses has been given to him by a Sovereign God purely by grace and mercy. Even the faith by which a man believes is **not of the man**, but is of God: **"For by grace are ye saved through faith; and that not of yourselves: IT IS THE GIFT OF GOD: not of works, lest any man should boast"** (Eph. 2:8,9; see also Acts 15:11; Gal. 3:22). Man has done, and could do, nothing to recommend himself unto God and can contribute nothing in order to make himself differ from any other man (Rom. 3:20,23). Any good deed or offering a lost man makes to God is unacceptable because it is imperfect and unclean, stained with sin. As was stated earlier, such blasphemous teachings as Christ dying for every individual, thus making salvation only possible and not effectual by His own atoning work on the Cross, controverts all that is taught in Scripture about what **atonement** actually is, which is what Christ went to the Cross to accomplish for His people. **The Bible knows nothing of an atonement made for sin which was dependant or conditioned on the sinner in any way, shape or form.** And those who promote such an atonement have absolutely **NO** support for it in Scripture. *"He who denies the penal and vicarious nature of Christ's death, repudiates the clear testimony of the types; he who sets aside the efficacy of His Sacrifice by reducing it to a merely 'making possible' the salvation of men does likewise, FOR THE TYPES KNOW NOTHING OF AN INEFFECTUAL SACRIFICE."* Atonement in the Bible was always made for God's chosen people and not for any others. **No one becomes a child of God by anything they do.** It is all because of what God does. Election, satisfaction for sin, a perfect righteousness, repentance from dead works and idolatry and the certainty that all whom God has chosen shall come to Him and remain with Him eternally, has all been the work of a Sovereign God and either given to, or performed on behalf of, the justified sinner. *"For whom He did foreknow, He also did predestinate to be conformed to the image of His Son, that He might be the Firstborn among many brethren. Moreover whom HE did predestinate, them HE also called: and whom HE called, them HE also justified: and whom HE justified, them HE also glorified"* (Rom. 8:29,30). God has done it all.

If one rightly holds to what the Bible teaches, that Christ died for His people, the elect of God, then one holds to the truth that what Christ did was actually **obtain redemption** for them by His death (Heb. 9:12). **Whoever Christ died for He has obtained eternal redemption.** This was dependant on Him and not in any way conditioned on the sinner, for all those who would receive what had been done on their behalf were chosen by God before the foundation of the world and given to the Son. God justifies the **ungodly** and not the godly (Rom. 4:5). Christ said He did not come to call the righteous but sinners to repentance (Matt. 9:13). No matter how religious and moral a person is, **no one is saved before they hear, understand and believe the Gospel of God. NO ONE IS BORN AGAIN UNLESS THEY ARE BORN OF THE GOSPEL!** To believe that one was saved before hearing the Gospel, that is, when the Gospel was hidden from them, which is to say when they were ignorant of Who Christ is and what Christ has done, is to base one's salvation on something other than God's Testimony and other than the Person and Work of God's only Son. **The Truth that is God's Gospel has yet to shine on them. Those who place their faith in anything other than the obedience and death of Jesus Christ ALONE, as meeting all the conditions for salvation from beginning to final glory, NOT MERELY DURING THEIR SO-CALLED SAVED STATE BUT RIGHT FROM ITS INCEPTION, have not God.** These are creatures who walk according to their natural state and are born, not of incorruptible Seed, but of corruptible seed. They are not spiritual creatures, that is, of the Spirit, but are of the flesh and do walk after the flesh.

The Gospel, or doctrine, of Christ is fundamentally as follows: man is dead in sin (Eph. 2:1,5), without God and without hope in the world (Eph. 2:12). This means that there is nothing in man that can lead him to the true God: **No man can come to Me, except the Father which hath sent Me draw him..."** and **"It is the Spirit that quickeneth; the flesh profiteth nothing..."** and **"...therefore said I unto you, that no man can come unto Me, except it were given unto him of My Father"** (Jn. 6:44,63,65). When asked who can be saved, the Lord Jesus replied **"...with men this is IMPOSSIBLE; but with God all things are possible"** (Matt. 19:26). This is in accord with the teaching just mentioned, that a man without God, and without the Gospel of God, is without hope. Man, if left to himself, has no hope of eternal salvation, of everlasting life. He does not know the Gospel, he does not know God and he does not know the way to God. **He is spiritually destitute!** The Bible says that **"...verily every man at his BEST state is altogether vanity"** (Psa. 39:5). It is God Who makes alive, purely by His Sovereign Will and Grace. Paul, speaking to believers, wrote: **"But God, Who is rich in mercy, for His great love wherewith He loved us, even when we were dead in sins, hath quickened us together with Christ, (by grace ye are saved;)"** (Eph. 2:4,5; see also Col. 2:13,14). **"...OF HIM are ye in Christ Jesus..."** (1 Cor. 1:30; see also 1 Pet. 1:21). God has chosen people from among every nation to be His people, His very own elected children (Rev. 5:9). God did this according to His Own Counsel. He did not confer with man nor did He act based on their *'good deeds'*. **God choosing those whom He would bless based on grace, is proof positive that man is dead in sin and cannot come to God by works or will.** All these are saved, not by means of their own obedience, but by the obedience of ONE (Rom. 5:19): **"Who hath saved us, and called us with an holy calling, not according to OUR WORKS, but according to His own purpose and grace, which was GIVEN us in Christ Jesus before the world began"** (2 Tim. 1:9), and not, as many so falsely teach, according to His foreknowledge of who would choose Him, for such an *'election'* would be according to a man's deeds and by reward, something which he has earned, rather than by God's purpose and grace. The Scriptures speak plainly: **"Now

to him that worketh is the reward not reckoned of grace, but of debt (Rom. 4:4; see also Rom. 6:23). It is Christ who has saved us and **"In Whom also we have obtained an inheritance, being predestinated according to the purpose of Him Who worketh all things after the counsel of His own will"**—not man's will (Eph. 1:11). The Bible says of Christians that the reason why God loves us is not because we loved Him first, **it is not we who have taken the initiative; it is not anything that we have done which has attracted God to us and prompted Him to love us and choose us** but **"We love Him, because He first loved us"** (1 Jn. 4:19 & v.10; see also Rom. 5:6,8).

The Lord Jesus paid the penalty of all the sins of all the elect of God whom God had given Him (Isa. 53:4,5) and has given them His Righteousness: **"Even as David also describeth the blessedness of the man, unto whom God imputeth righteousness WITHOUT WORKS"** (Rom. 4:6; see also 4:8). The righteousness which is given a man is not a reward for anything the man has done, for then it could not be called a salvation purely of grace, but is freely imputed, or charged, by God's grace based on the obedience of Another: Christ Jesus the Lord: **"And if by grace, then is it no more of works: otherwise grace is no more grace. But if it be of works, then is it no more grace: otherwise work is no more work"** (Rom. 11:6). God's Justice is satisfied, for the penalty which the sins of God's elect had earned has been met, **and could only have been met,** in full by Christ alone: **"Christ hath redeemed us from the curse of the law, being made a curse for us: for it is written, cursed is everyone that hangeth on a tree"** (Gal. 3:13). We shall be presented to God faultless, spotless and blameless (Jude 24 & Col. 1:22) for we are robed with Christ's perfect Righteousness and not in the filthy rags of righteousnesses which are of our own making (Isa. 64:6): **"I will greatly rejoice in the Lord, my soul shall be joyful in my God; for He hath clothed me with the garments of salvation, He hath covered me with the Robe of Righteousness..."** (Isa. 61:10). Jesus Christ alone has also *fully* met the requirements of God's Holy law, by His perfect obedience:

"For as by one man's disobedience many were made sinners, so BY THE OBEDIENCE OF ONE shall many be made righteous" (Rom. 5:19). The elect referred to here as the *many*, will not be made righteous because of their own individual and imperfect adherence to God's commands, but are made righteous by the obedience of One: **Jesus Christ, the Lord of Glory!** All of God's elect will hear the Gospel and will, at the appointed time, believe it for this has been predetermined by God's immutable Counsel and Will (Acts 13:48; see also 2:47). And the Bible teaches that all for whom this has been done will never perish (Jn. 10:27:28; see also Jn. 6:37-40). They have been saved eternally and are preserved in Christ (Jude 1 & Psa. 37:28). The blood of Christ has not provided a temporary state of salvation for whom it was shed, but it has **ETERNALLY** saved all for whom it was shed. **Their sins have been wiped out, their debt has been paid in full and a perfect Righteousness established and imputed unto them** (see Rom. 4:6-8). The salvation that a Christian has is not one which is conditioned on his efforts at obedience, and therefore subject to change, for then no one could be saved, but is conditioned on Christ from **beginning to end** and is therefore eternal and wavers not. The saved man is not kept saved by his efforts but by the power of God through faith in Christ (1 Pet. 1:5; see also Jn. 17:11,12). To believe otherwise is to deny the efficaciousness of Christ's atoning death and Christ's finished work being sufficient, not only to save His people, but to ensure the **eternal** security of those people. **To deny the Work of Christ is to deny the Person of Christ and to deny Him is to deny His Father's Testimony of Who He is and what He has done, as revealed in the Gospel.** *"Whosoever denieth the Son, the same hath not the Father: [but] he that acknowledgeth the Son hath the Father also"* (1 Jn.2:23). Just as those who deny the Son do not have the Father, so, too, those who do not stand in Christ's doctrine do not have either the Son or the Father (2 John 9).

The life every true born of the Gospel believer now has is *everlasting life*, which means that, not only will they live forever, but they have, by the grace of God, **been made**

alive unto Him eternally. THERE IS NO SIN THAT CAN UNDO THIS, FOR CHRIST HAS BLOTTED OUT THE BELIEVER'S SINS, HAVING NAILED THEM TO THE CROSS! (Col. 2:13-15). EVERY SIN OF EVERY BELIEVER HAS BEEN MET, DEALT WITH AND FORGIVEN, FOR CHRIST DIED FOR ALL THE SINS OF EVERY BELIEVER AND HAS CARRIED THEM AWAY. If every sin of every believer has been atoned for, would it not be right to conclude that the sin of unbelief, that sin which for so long kept the believer from God and in a dead spiritual state, has also been taken out of the way? And if not, then the sin of unbelief has not been done away with for the elect and there is no atonement for it. The penalty it has incurred has not been paid and therefore no one can possibly come to God, for the sin of unbelief reigns supreme, being untouched by the blood of Christ. How ludicrous all this is in light of what God says in His Holy Word. Has not Christ suffered the penalty of all the sins of the elect, including the sin of unbelief? **If so, how could anyone for whom Christ has suffered, possibly die in unbelief and dead to God when the penalty for that very sin of unbelief has already been paid by the Lord Jesus?**

God will never leave His chosen people nor forsake them (see Psa. 37:28 & Heb. 13:5) and because of this, they will never leave Him or forsake Him. The seed of man might give life but it is a temporal life and it is corruptible seed from which it is brought forth, which means that it will one day perish. **However, all that spring from the Seed of God have a spiritual life which is eternal and will never perish, for that Seed which they have been born out of—the Gospel—is incorruptible.** Christ said it this way: **"That which is born of the flesh is flesh; and that which is born of the Spirit is spirit"** (Jn. 3:6). This means that that which is born of the flesh, that is, man's natural sinful nature, cannot but be natural and sinful itself and will one day die. The Pharisee, Nicodemus, who had just asked if what Jesus meant by the phrase **"...except a man be born again..."** (Jn. 3:3,4) that a man must enter a second time into his mother's womb did not understand what Christ had said. Even if a man could re-enter his mother's womb *"He would still be possessed by the same natural propensities and* *passions....*(that which is of the flesh) (He) *Partakes of the nature of the parent. As the parents are corrupt and sinful, so will be their descendants. And as the parents are wholly corrupt by nature, so their children will be the same. The word 'flesh' here is used to denote 'corrupt, defiled, sinful.'"* On the other hand, that which is born of the Spirit of God, or by the agency of the Holy Spirit through the means of the Gospel of God, is spirit as well. Only the born again man will see the Kingdom of Heaven. *"Here we learn that all men are by nature sinful. That none are renewed but by the Spirit of God. If man did the work himself* (or contributed in any way to any degree), *it would be still flesh, and impure."* **Man must be born again; he must be born of that incorruptible Seed; he must be born of the Gospel if he is to see the Kingdom of God.**

None of God's children believe anything less, or more, than this simple Gospel as the only way to salvation. Christ said He is the Way to the Father: *"...I am the Way, the Truth, and the Life: no man cometh unto the Father, but by Me"* (Jn. 14:6; see also Heb. 7:25). Also, *"Neither is there salvation in any other: for there is none other name under heaven given among men, whereby we must be saved"* (Acts 4:12). The way **to** God is not a life of good works, for the Bible says that by works shall no flesh be justified (Gal. 2:16). **Good works will be a fruit of salvation, but are not a contributing factor or the means to anyone's justification** (see 2 Tim. 1:9). A man is saved purely by God Himself choosing the man to be saved, **by means of his hearing, understanding and believing His Gospel**. All who abide in the doctrine of Christ are preserved in Christ (Jude 1) and their inheritance is reserved for them in heaven. According to the abundant mercy of God, and not our works, HE *"...hath BEGOTTEN US AGAIN unto a lively hope by the Resurrection of Jesus Christ from the dead, to an inheritance incorruptible, and undefiled, and that fadeth not away, reserved in heaven for you, who are kept by the power of God through faith UNTO salvation ready to be revealed in the last time"* (1 Pet. 1:3-5). All who reject the doctrine of Christ have not God and shall be eternally damned if they remain in that state: **"Whosoever transgresseth, and ABIDETH NOT IN THE DOCTRINE OF CHRIST, HATH NOT GOD. He that ABIDETH in the doctrine of Christ, he HATH both the Father and the Son. If there come ANY unto you and bring not THIS DOCTRINE, receive him not into your house, neither bid him God speed: For he that biddeth him God speed is partaker of his evil deeds"** (2 Jn. 9-11).

The Gospel that has been presented to you in this booklet is the one that many claim to believe in. This writer has been privileged to preach this message and tell others about it on numerous occasions via letters, emails, booklets and both video and audio tapes of my own and of others. Yet most of those I know who have never heard this message in its entirety before, insist that though they believe this message now, they were nonetheless saved before they heard it. **Saved in ignorance of the Gospel they now claim to believe! Such people clearly do not understand what they say they believe.** They are blind to the fact that this Gospel shuts out all who do not believe it and who say they were saved before hearing it. Many say that this is the Gospel they have believed in for years, even decades, yet they become offended when it is defined for them in finer detail. **They are familiar with Christian terminology, but not with the meaning.** This reveals to me the sad and decaying state they are currently in. It shows that while they are certainly conversant with most terms intrinsic to the Gospel, they haven't a clue as to their real meaning. **The Gospel simply has not been revealed to them.** When such terms are properly and biblically explained to them, they flee in terror uttering accusatory terms such as *'cult!', 'extremist!', evil teaching!', 'unloving!'* etc. This writer has had people ask for items promoting this Gospel, for a time, and even ordering multiple copies of my own tapes and booklets, and yet all of a sudden their communication comes to an abrupt halt after the penny finally drops and the realisation comes upon them like a blast from a fiery furnace that this Message pronounces them lost before they claim to have believed this Gospel, and, therefore, still in a lost state for they believe in a salvation without the Gospel. The True

Gospel is something they cannot bear to contemplate and so they trample off into the sunset with a firm hold on their beliefs, all the while ignorant of or in denial of the fact that their feet tread the path described in Scripture as the broad way that only leads one away from God to destruction (Matt. 7:13).

One cannot make the message any clearer than is humanly possible. Only God can make a person see it in its fullness and receive it. But allow me to make the following statements so that none can confuse what I am saying, or accuse me of being vague or that my writings are obscure and that I do not make the message clear enough; that I do not make a distinct sound when I blow the warning trumpet:

NO MAN IS SAVED WHO DOES NOT BELIEVE THIS GOSPEL IN ITS ENTIRETY.

NO MAN IS SAVED WHO BELIEVES THAT ANYONE ELSE, REGARDLESS OF APPEARANCE OR REPUTATION, IS SAVED WHILST BELIEVING ANY OTHER GOSPEL.

NO MAN IS SAVED WHO BELIEVES THAT HE, OR ANYONE ELSE, WAS SAVED BEFORE THEY HEARD AND BELIEVED THIS GOSPEL.

No one ever arrived at their destination before they actually got there! So, too, no one was ever saved BEFORE they heard and believed THE Gospel of Jesus Christ: *"But though we, or an angel from heaven, preach any other gospel unto you than that which we have preached unto you, LET HIM BE ACCURSED"* (Gal. 1:8). Paul here tells of the accursed state of any man who teaches, and therefore anyone who believes in, another gospel. Isaiah puts it this way: *"To the Law and to the Testimony: if they speak not according to this Word, IT IS BECAUSE THERE IS NO LIGHT IN THEM"* (Isa. 8:20). How can he be saved who has not placed his trust in the only One Who can save and Who has revealed Himself only in the Gospel? **Every true** righteousness of his own, sure and conclusive evidence that he was ignorant of and not submitted to the only Righteousness that can make a man just before God—**the Righteousness of Christ!** Paul was comforted during his ignorant Christless religious life by his efforts at obeying God's commands and producing what he thought were good works. These so-called good works, which Paul counted as nothing but dung after he heard the Gospel, the True Way to salvation, were nothing but a false refuge which gave Paul a false sense of peace and security when it came to the matter of his eternal destiny. Where is that Message of the Righteousness of Christ, which most professing Christians are ignorant of, revealed? **Nowhere else but in the Gospel of God, His Incorruptible Seed.** Paul never found, or had, salvation before he heard and believed in the Gospel of God. With all his religion and all his Jewish ancestry, Paul was as lost as the heathen **for he knew not Christ and abided not in His doctrine**. And, please, do not for one moment think that Paul, or should I say Saul, back in his lost days was different to those who claim to be saved today because he did not believe that Jesus was the Messiah, as all who would claim to be Christian today do. Though Paul did not believe Jesus was the Messiah, he did believe in a counterfeit Messiah. He believed in another messiah whom he thought was the real Messiah and who he believed was still to come. Paul believed in another jesus (messiah) and another gospel just as much as those today who hold to a false gospel that promotes a counterfeit christ.

"*DO YOU HAVE A RIGHTEOUSNESS THAT ANSWERS THE DEMANDS OF GOD'S HOLY LAW AND JUSTICE? It is impossible for any sinner to have it based on character and conduct. If anyone has it, it is only by imputation, God freely giving it. We then receive it by faith*" (WP).

The Scriptures speak plainly for all to understand: **"Whosoever transgresseth, and abideth not in the doctrine of Christ, HATH NOT GOD. He that abideth in the doctrine of Christ, HE HATH BOTH THE FATHER AND THE SON"** (2 Jn. 9). The Scriptures speak equally as clear in 1 Peter when they state that **to be born again one must be born of incorruptible Seed: the Gospel of God**. To those who do not receive the True Christ of God's ONLY Gospel, the One Who has already come and Who will come again, Jesus Christ says: **"And ye have not this Word abiding in you: for Whom He hath sent, Him ye believe not....ye have not the love of God in you. I am come in My Father's name and ye receive Me not..."** (Jn. 5:38, 42,43). **"If any man love not THE Lord Jesus Christ, let him be anathema** (accursed)" (1 Cor. 16:22). If any do not believe and obey the Gospel they are lost. If any are not born again they are lost. And if any are not born of the Word of Truth, that Mighty Gospel Seed of God, **they are lost**! Christ Jesus says: **"The time is fulfilled, and the Kingdom of God is at hand: repent ye, and BELIEVE THE GOSPEL"** (Mk. 1:15).

"If there come ANY unto you, and bring not THIS DOCTRINE, receiveth him not into your house, neither bid him God speed: For he that biddeth him God speed is partaker of his evil deeds" (2 Jn.10, 11).

Made in the USA
Monee, IL
03 May 2026

49437985R00036